Contents

William Collins' dream of knowledge for all began with the publication of his first book in 1819.
A self-educated mill worker, he not only enriched millions of lives, but also founded a flourishing publishing house.
Today, staying true to this spirit, Collins books are packed with inspiration, innovation and practical expertise.
They place you at the centre of a world of possibility and give you exactly what you need to explore it.

Collins. Freedom to teach.

Published by Collins
An imprint of HarperCollins*Publishers*
The News Building, 1 London Bridge Street, London, SE1 9GF, UK

HarperCollins*Publishers*
Macken House, 39/40 Mayor Street Upper, Dublin 1, DO1 C9W8, Ireland

> Browse the complete Collins catalogue at
> **www.collins.co.uk**

British Library Cataloguing-in-Publication Data
A catalogue record for this publication is available from the British Library.

Compiled by: Fiona Macgregor
Publisher: Elaine Higgleton
Product manager: Letitia Luff
Commissioning editor: Rachel Houghton
Edited by: Hannah Hirst-Dunton
Editorial management: Oriel Square
Cover designer: Kevin Robbins
Cover illustrations: Jouve India Pvt. Ltd.
Additional text credit: p 3–9 Alison Hawes, p 10–21 An Vrombaut, p 24–29 Paul Shipton
Internal illustrations: p 3–9 Manya Stojic, p 10–21 An Vrombaut, p 24–29 John Gordon
Typesetter: Jouve India Pvt. Ltd.
Production controller: Lyndsey Rogers
Printed and bound in the UK using 100% Renewable Electricity at Martins the Printers

MIX
Paper | Supporting responsible forestry
FSC™ C007454

This book is produced from independently certified FSC™ paper to ensure responsible forest management.

For more information visit: www.harpercollins.co.uk/green

Acknowledgements

With thanks to all the kindergarten staff and their schools around the world who have helped with the development of this course, by sharing insights and commenting on and testing sample materials:

Calcutta International School: Sharmila Majumdar, Mrs Pratima Nayar, Preeti Roychoudhury, Tinku Yadav, Lakshmi Khanna, Mousumi Guha, Radhika Dhanuka, Archana Tiwari, Urmita Das; Gateway College (Sri Lanka): Kousala Benedict; Hawar International School: Kareen Barakat, Shahla Mohammed, Jennah Hussain; Manthan International School: Shalini Reddy; Monterey Pre-Primary: Adina Oram; Prometheus School: Aneesha Sahni, Deepa Nanda; Pragyanam School: Monika Sachdev; Rosary Sisters High School: Samar Sabat, Sireen Freij, Hiba Mousa; Solitaire Global School: Devi Nimmagadda; United Charter Schools (UCS): Tabassum Murtaza and staff; Vietnam Australia International School: Holly Simpson

The publishers wish to thank the following for permission to reproduce photographs.

(t = top, c = centre, b = bottom, r = right, l = left)

p 3 FAN travelstock/Alamy, p 4 david sanger photography/Alamy, p 5 Jenny Tobias/Corbis, p 6 Roland Liptak/Alamy, p 7 Cindy Kassab/Corbis, p 8 Joanne Moyes/Alamy, p 22t Evgeny Atamanenko/Shutterstock, p 22c ALPA PROD/Shutterstock, p 22b Sahacha Nilkumhang/Shutterstock, p 23t Kzenon/Shutterstock, p 23b fizkes/Shutterstock, p 30t Bigbubblebee99/Shutterstock, p 30c George Rudy/Shutterstock, p 30b TY Lim/Shutterstock, p 31t Aleksandr Khmeliov/Shutterstock, p 31b wavebreakmedia/Shutterstock

The weather report

It was sunny on Sunday.

It was cloudy on Monday.

It was rainy on Tuesday.

It was windy on Wednesday.

It was foggy on Thursday.

It was snowy on Friday
and Saturday.

Sunday

Monday

Tuesday

Wednesday

Thursday

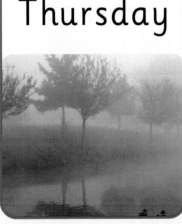

Friday
Saturday

Duck socks

Hip has duck socks.

Hip has red dot socks.

Hop has duck socks.

One has red dots. One has no red dots.

Hop is a sad duck.

Hip gets a red sack.

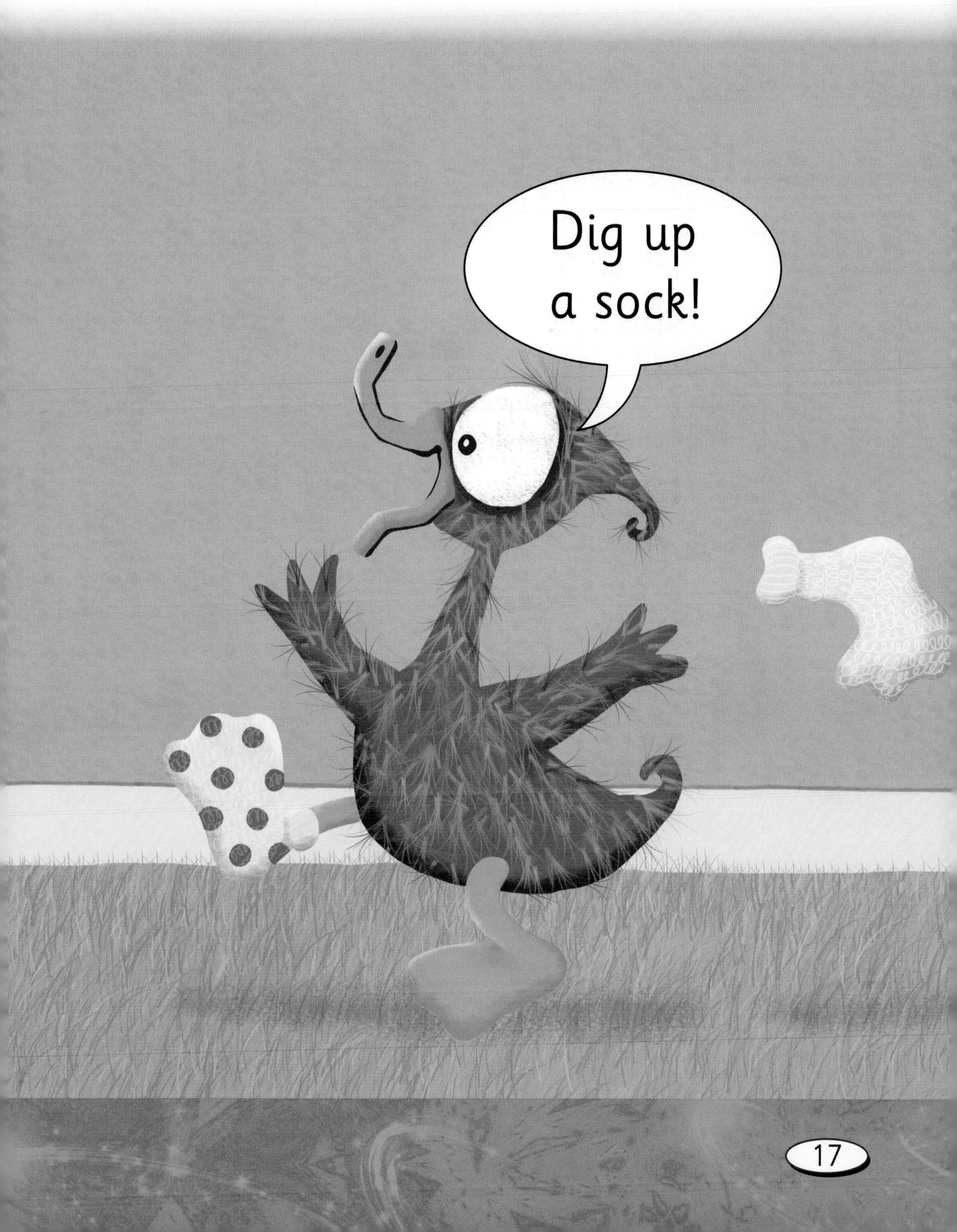
Dig up a sock!

Hop digs up a sock.

It is a red dot sock!

Hop has red dot socks.

Red dot socks rock!

What is my job?

Susan is a pilot. She flies a helicopter.

Chris is a singer. He sings songs.

Dirk is a driver. He drives this big truck!

Busi is a writer. She writes books for children.

The farmer's lunch

SURPRISE!

What can you do?

I can use a phone. What can you do?

I can use a computer. What can you do?

I can use a tablet. What can you do?

I can use a camera. What can you do?

Reading notes

Story	Sounds	Language structures
The weather report	'r', 'o'	Describing the weather: *It was … on …*; using weather words and days of the week
Duck socks	'h', 'k'	Saying what one has: *I have/he has/she has*
What is my job?	'j', 'o', 'b'	Discussing jobs: *He is a…, She is a…*
The farmer's lunch	'l', 'u', 'm', 'y'	Describing where things are: *It is on/in/under the…*; using the word *my*
What can you do?	revision	Identifying what you can do: *I can use a… What can you do?*

When you read these stories to your children at home, point out the new sound(s) in each story. Encourage your child to find the letter on the page. Then get them to say the sound, and the word, out loud.

Practise these language structures by asking questions. For example, ask: *What is the weather today?* to elicit the response: *It is rainy*, or ask: *What can you do?* to get the answer: *I can use a computer.*